Laughter

Laughter Lines

James McCormick

The Pentland Press Limited
Edinburgh • Cambridge • Durham • USA

First published in 1998 by
The Pentland Press Ltd.
1 Hutton Close
South Church
Bishop Auckland
Durham

British Library Cataloguing in Publication Data.
A Catalogue record for this book is available
from the British Library.

ISBN 1 85821 633 8

Typeset by CBS, Martlesham Heath, Ipswich, Suffolk
Printed and bound by Antony Rowe Ltd., Chippenham

FOREWORD

by

JOHN BOYLE

Chairman: MOTHERWELL F.C.
Chairman: DIRECT HOLIDAYS
Chairman: DIRECT CRUISES

I first met Jimmy McCormick in 1967 when he was a teacher in Holy Cross High School, Hamilton and I was starting Fifth Year.

He was most approachable as a teacher and showed a ready understanding of pupils' problems.

He would, always, try to put the best interpretation on any situation. He was slow to condemn and quick to praise. He was not a stern disciplinarian but his quiet authority was respected. Always willing to give people, myself included, a second or even a third chance.

His classes were successful, his lessons, informative and effective. Important points were emphasised with an apposite anecdote, often humorous, which ensured the lesson was understood and remembered.

As Head of Upper School, he was responsible each year, God help him! for two hundred diverse, intelligent, opinionated, hormonally explosive seventeen and eighteen year olds, all anxious to make their way in life and their mark on society.

His written references, whilst honest, always accentuated the positive elements in a pupil's character. Many successful people today, were helped to their first step on the industrial, commercial, academic or professional ladder by his complimentary comments on their application forms.

He acted as a liberal, supervisory editor and censor to a daringly, alternative school newspaper called 'CROSSFIRE' produced by myself and a number of fellow pupils. One of his happier tasks was to judge the 'MISS CROSSFIRE' contest. This was before the onset of POLITICAL CORRECTNESS.

This group has maintained a close friendship with each other and with Jimmy, since leaving school thirty years ago.

I had the pleasure of inviting many of his family and friends to a party, in my home, on Hogmanay 1995 to celebrate his 70th birthday.

He was always a popular speaker at Presentations, Burns Suppers and school reunions, and this may have been the catalyst which sparked off his writing.

His friends have long been amused by his clever verses. I am pleased to be associated, even in a small way, with the book which brings this enjoyment to a larger audience.

The verses, like himself, are without malice. They are written for fun – and funny they are. Reactions range from a wry smile through a quiet giggle to outright laughter. By their very variety of subjects, they show the same combination of familiarity with a wide range of topics, a facility with words and a warmth and wit which characterised his teaching.

Here are 'LAUGHTER LINES' – enjoy – I did.

JOHN BOYLE
KINNELL HOUSE

THE GOOD SAMARITAN 90s VERSION

Rolling home from the pub, 'weel smugged,'
Wullie, was well and truly mugged.
On his midnight stroll through Kelvin Way,
A place, quite safe by light of day,
He was waylaid by a six foot nutter,
Who left him bleeding in the gutter.
The first to pass and see him lie,
Dark suit, striped shirt and Old School Tie,
A stockbroker he, on Glasgow Market,
In rather superior tones remarkit,
From the safety and comfort of his Merc
'Don't he knaow naights er dangerous in the Perk.'
Fast, decisive action the crisis meets,
'Just think of the blood on my leather seats,
What he got, he must have deserved,
And, moral values must be preserved.'
Smugly, he drove into the night,
Confident he had maintained the Right.
The next – who, the flesh pots, had abjured –
A Vegan, Marxist, wee shop steward,
A riveter's hauder-oan to trade,
Was, by this sight, fell dismayed,
'This is Society's retribution
For unfair economic distribution.'
Quickly sizing up the situation,
Saw this as a case of demarcation,
It might be for medics or undertakers,
But, certainly not for the Boilermakers.
So, having averted a possible strike,
Pedalled off on his ozone-friendly, bike.
A Social Worker hove in sight,
Ideals in place and honour bright,
He watched documentaries on Granada,
And drove a small, beige coloured Lada.

A Fair Isle pully, a crocheted tie,
His Oxfam suit, the best that he could buy.
He'd left a job that pays one better,
Compassion was his raison d'être.
Professional training must show through,
Directly, he saw what he must do.
Driving off, he knew the die was cast,
'Whoever did this, needs my help, fast.'

* * *

Swiss watches are precisely made
They function to perfection,
The Swiss Guards, when they're on parade,
Provide the Pope's protection.

Swiss army knives have blades galore,
Their banks are confidential,
Of languages, the Swiss have four,
Their wealth is exponential.

Headwaters of the Rhine and Rhône,
Yodelling from peak to peak,
Cheese with holes and Toblerone,
Muesli seven days a week.

Five hundred years of peace they've had,
To contemplate the view.
In no way are the Swiss folk mad,
But their clocks are all cuckoo.

* * *

Said the vicar to his verger, 'I'm very cross,
Someone's stolen my bike and I mourn its loss,
But, like Baldrick, I have a cunning plan,
On Sunday, you will, the congregation, scan.
On the Ten Commandments, I shall preach,
And when, 'Thou shalt not steal' I reach,
Watch, closely, each parishioner's face
And if, of guilt, there is a trace,
As soon as the services are done,
Report to me on the suspect one.'

But the plan's execution was, somewhat, desultory,
And the conclusion, one he did not much like,
As he reached 'Thou shalt not commit adultery',
He remembered where he'd left his bike.

* * *

The farmer 'phoned his local veterinary pool,
'It's happened, again, to my prize stud bull.
I've tried him with all the best cows on the farm,
But the sexual dynamo just can't perform.
It happened before, but the vet put him right,
With pills that were coloured, a green stripe on white.
I don't know what they're called but they're made out of paste,
And, as well, they'd a quite pleasant peppermint taste.'

THE ORIGIN OF YODELLING
Canto 1

'The shades of night were falling fast,
When through an Alpine village passed.'
A knight, returned from the Crusade,
Who, on his lance, a note displayed
Which, in Ye Olde English, said,
'I neede my supper and a bedde.'
Upspoke a lass, in dirndl wear,
'There's room for thee and thy brindle mare.
My mother and father keep the inn,
And goodly fare is served therein.'
She led him up the mountain side
There, on a ledge, just ten yards wide,
The inn, with smoking chimney, stood,
Fashioned, with care, from local wood.
A balcony, built in days of yore,
Gave views right down the valley floor,
Beneath the steep, o'erhanging eaves,
The winter's logs were stacked, like sheaves.
A cow, with bell of copper made,
Was kept there for the tourist trade,
The local artist, so it seems,
Would paint you, patting it, for a few centimes.

Canto 2

Proudly, on the step, stood Mine Host Anton,
(He'd the biggest Alpenhorn in the Canton),
Broad braces with embroidered clocks,
Leder hosen and knee-high socks.
He looked at the knight, a mite suspicious,
He knew his daughter was capricious,
Last week a flash French troubadour,
Singing roundelays round the door.
The week before, a costumed jester,
Who, with wise saws, sought ways to best her,
Only his utmost concentration,
Prevented his daughter's defloration.
Looking at the knight's bright shield,
A slogan was, thereon, revealed,
By the light of a candle, in its sconce,
Read 'Honi Soit Qui Mal Y Pense.'
Anton, who'd read his Magna Carta,
Knew this as the motto of the Garter.
(Meanwhile his wife, with sidelong glance,
Admired the phallic symbol of his lance.)
'Sir, a KNIGHT'S lodging here I seek.'
(Pleased with his pun, though rather weak.)
'I'll be off with a LARK, 'ere day's begun.'
(Was this a promise or another pun?)
"I'll be on with my MAIL ere your POST is PAST. '
(The puns were now coming, thick and fast.)
'This KNIGHT-MARE pair will you SWISS MISS.'
(Oh! better the jester, than more of this.)
'Lodging we'll gladly grant you here,
With the best of food and butts of beer.
Welcome to my inn – but Zounds!
My daughter's room is out of bounds.'
'On that you may put me to the TEST,
An Englishman differs from the rest.

The act of BOWLING A MAIDEN OVER,
Has another meaning north of Dover.
A SLIP, MID OFF, FINE LEG, CAUGHT BEHIND,
Bring only the game of cricket to mind.
'Ere leaving my wife, we made a pact,
We would, our virtues, keep intact.
In fact, to show the trust I felt,
I gave a friend the key of her chastity belt.
For your welcome, you must be thanked,
Your daughter's boudoir is sacrosanct.'
They knew Crusaders were not TOO rich,
(This was before the Gnomes of Zurich.)
So, on payment of a pittance,
The goodly Knight has gained admittance.

Canto 3

As promised, supper was a fine repast,
With courses numerous and vast,
Soup made from a real ox-tail,
Accompanied by large steins of ale,
Haunch of venison, from a local deer,
Washed down with copious draughts of beer,
A sweet white wine, straight from the wood'll,
Complement the hostess's apple strudel.
A Swiss cheese, eaten with his dagger,
Delicious, with a home-brewed lager.
Supper over and grace been said,
The ladies soon retired to bed.
'Good-night,' said Anton to his guest,
But, just to set his mind at rest,
Pulled a chair across the wooden floor,
And sat outside his daughter's door,
Ready for whate'er mayhap,

Held a loaded cross-bow on his lap.
But, heavy with good food and booze,
Soon, head on chest, began to snooze,
Thus allowing our martial cavalier,
To behave like any commercial traveller.
After – what we must just assume –
He left the lovely lass's room.
Noting Anton still asleep,
As quietly as he could creep,
Aimed for the room across the way
Wherein his handsome hostess lay.

Canto 4

Daylight, through the window, streaming,
Woke Anton from his pleasant dreaming,
Dashing to his daughter's bed,
A smile upon her face he read.
'Daughter! Daughter! are you alright?
Did something happen through the night?'
She, with a glint in her blue eye,
Hesitated to reply.
He knew, quite well, from this hiatus,
His daughter had lost her virgin status.
From the balcony, as he had feared,
Down on the valley floor appeared,
The knight, his armour in disorder,
Galloping headlong for the border.
'Come back!' The anguished father cried,
Words echoed down the mountain side.
'Thy scheming English ways have caught her,
You have seduced my lovely daughter.'
The knight, as he disappeared from view,
Called back, 'AND YOORE OLD LADEE TOO.'

7

TEACHER'S LAMENT

To ease the stress of class 3c,
Two solutions there seem to be:
Either a frontal lobotomy,
Or a bottle in front of me.

* * *

How many times has it been said
The sweetest sweets are those, purloined?
There – in the pre-nuptial bed,
To be joyfully loined 'ere lawfully joined.

* * *

Florists' economics are rather funny,
'THRIFT' costs the customer extra money,
Their morality, too, is somewhat strange,
The sell their 'HONESTY' for small change.

* * *

Oysters are aphrodisiac, they say,
But I am feeling irked,
I ate a dozen yesterday,
And only seven worked.

One day, for money, Ed Manet ,
Went to paint Claude Monet's old granny,
Think what that painting would be worth today,
Except that old granny had just passed away.

* * *

Here's the E.N.T. surgeon's joke.
The removal of a POLYP would evoke.
'Reflect on the rim of a bed-pan, do,
For it, after all, is a PO LIP too.'

* * *

A Scottish priest, hearing Confessions in Paris,
Didn't permit his lack of French, to embarrass.
Though, only understanding a word or two,
He'd say, sternly, "Oh! Vous AVEZ – avez vous?"

* * *

Fewer pounds for his yen in negotiations,
The Japanese tourist made quite a to-do.
'Sir,' said the bank clerk, 'It's fluctuations.'
'In which case,' said he, 'Fluct you Europeans too.'

* * *

In the Old Folk's Home a new doctor and minister,
Were both appointed at the very same time.
One came to old Jeannie, his skills to administer,
A lady still, mentally, well in her prime.
'You're fine,' said the nurse, 'That's the doctor's belief,
His examination shows nothing sinister.'
'Oh! the DOCTOR,' said Jeannie, with obvious relief,
'Ah thocht he was ower fameeliar for a minister.'

* * *

The building site foreman was swearing blue murder.
As the, vacation work, student he attempted to oust.
'What's the B__ difference between a joist and a girder?'
'Easy – JOYCE wrote "*ULYSSES*" and GOETHE wrote "*FAUST*".'

BURNS' ODE ON THE PASSING OF THE MINI-SKIRT

(In which, our poet, Mr Robert Burns, waxes lyrical in praise of the Mini-skirt, bemoans its passing and, later rejoices in its reappearance, in even briefer form, in the 90s.)

Wee primped and painted dolly burdies,
Ah loo'e the skirt that girds yir hurdies,
Made frae stuff that cost twa curdies,
An' nane tae spare,
Gars men's heids burl like hurdie-gurdies,
And stop and stare.

It's shair a sign o' man's dominion,
That each fat lass, an' eke a thin yin,
Will eagerly display a pinion,
Tae catch men's glances,
And think that o' a legal union,
Her chance enhances.

In these much mair permissive days,
I'd spent my time in different ways,
And no' writ a' they odes an' lays
On mooses hooses,
But cast a lang, poetic gaze,
On see-through blooses.

Whit stirrin' times tae be a lad,
Here wis a sicht, the hert tae glad,
In froth o' frilly knickers clad,
Baith pink an' blue,
And, leanin' owre, each lassie had,
An end in view.

But skirts and time were short, like fame,
An' watchin' lassies is noo quite tame,
Fur Crash! the cruel Midi came,
Tae blight the view,
An' connoisseurs o' wimmen's frame,
Are oan the b'roo.

Perhaps the future's no' sae dusty,
Fur lads whose outlook, still, is lusty,
A fittin' end tae Midi, musty,
We're sure tae get.
Yince mair, ere memories get rusty,
The Mini's back, an shorter yet!

GLOSSARY

If, to you, this Burnsian Ode,
Seems written in a secret code,
And, should a glossary you seek,
A 'HURDIE' is your 'BOTTOM'S CHEEK'.
In case you think it's rather wordy,
A 'FARTHING', in Scots, is called a 'CURDIE',
If 'BURL' catches you upon the hop,
It means 'TO SPIN' – just like a top.
As Orpheus' lute charmed 'BIRDS' or 'BURDIES',
'BARREL ORGANS' are 'HURDIE-GURDIES',
The man, of sexy view, devoid,
Is 'OAN THE B'ROO' – he's 'UNEMPLOYED'.
(It comes from 'Bureau of Employment' I guess,
Now replaced by the DSS.)

BURNS REVISED

'Come fetch tae me a pint o' wine,
And fill it in a silver tassie,'
Iron Brew wid dae jist fine,
But isn't half sae middle classie.

* * *

Thanks for the giftie, some poo'er has gi'en us.
The pill's ta'en the fricht oot the sport o' Venus.

* * *

THE BIGOT

'For a' that and a' that, a man's a man micht be,
But denominational integration is, simply, no' for me.'
So, each conciliatory overture, RELIGIOUSLY, he spurns.
Even the ecumenic candle, some progressive RABBI BURNS.

* * *

OBSERVATION ON A TAXI OVERCHARGING

By charging more than should the fare be,
To retaliate, did that taxi dare me.
No wonder he was feeling huffed,
'Cos TAXIDERMY, means 'Get stuffed.'

Disturbed, in her bath, by a knock on the door,
Naked – she dripped water all over the floor.
'Who's there?' she asked, prepared to retreat.
'I'm an old blind salesman trying to make ends meet.'
So she opened the door – and he gave out a yell,
'It looks like you need the BLINDS that I sell.'

* * *

Lines on being given the present of a thimble with a picture on it of the MANNEKIN PIS (Fountain in Brussels with the statue of a wee boy, weeing.)

Don't TACK the NEEDLE or lose the HEAD,
You'll be in STITCHES, if you follow the THREAD.
SEW his EYE and wit would SEAM REEL nimble,
He COTTON to this POINT – it's a PHALLIC THIMBLE.

* * *

A spinster, seeking to lose weight,
Wants a double helping hand from fate.
Firstly she is trying to diet,
And second, of course, she is dying to try it.

* * *

Moses came down from the Mount, in troth,
Stone Tablets in his hand.
'I've good news and I've bad news both.'
Said he to the waiting Jewish band.
'I've got Him down to ten, as sin.
Sadly, adultery is still in.'

(Great wailings and lamentations.)

* * *

GAY PAREE

Chopin's Fourth Impromptu, that lovely air,
Was much admired by Baudelaire,
But, somewhat less in Verlaine prose.
Though he was always chasing Rimbauds.

* * *

BOPPIN' CHOPIN

In Majorca, CHOPIN,
Got his backside tanned,
From lying, naked,
On top of SAND.

'LET THE (BRIDAL) TRAIN TAKE THE STRAIN'

Shashi Patel had a reputation,
As the best restaurateur in Hamilton town.
One day he approached the railway station,
Carrying his best, silk wedding gown,
He had a letter from his father to say,
That he had arranged a wonderful marriage,
To a girl from a village just east of Bombay,
And that he should depart by the first railway carriage.

'May I have a single to Chandragorri?'
He asked of the clerk behind the wicket.
'I can't book for there, I'm very sorry,
I can get you to Glasgow, here is the ticket.'
At Glasgow he made the same request,
But was told there was nothing they could do.
'I really think it would be best,
To travel to London – Waterloo.'

At Waterloo he fared no better,
They said, too, they were sorry, very,
Never heard of the village in the letter,
So sent him to Dover, and the ferry.
At Calais, he received bad news,
No matter quite how long it took,
That, if the train he wished to use,
Each separate stage he'd have to book.

Paris, Prague and Budapest,
Byala, Belgrade and Bucharest,
Ankara via Istanbul,
Tabriz, Tehran and then Kabul.
The River Indus, he crosses o'er,
To reach the city of Lahore.
From Delhi to Ahmadabad,

Where he is met by his fond dad,
They take the first train to Bombay,
And reach the village late next day.

The wedding was a grand affair,
The bride was very much to his taste,
Soon, though, they had to prepare
For their return – no time to waste.

He said, 'My Dearest, we must hurry,
I must get back to the Mumtaz, quick,
They'll miss my very special curry,
No one else quite knows the trick.'

A whitewashed shack, was the railway station,
The porter sported a cotton vest.
'I'll book you straight through to your destination,
Was it Hamilton Central or Hamilton West?'

PRETENTIOUS – ? MOI – ?

If you say 'A STRATA'
When you mean one 'STRATUM',
You're not committing 'AN ERRATA',
But a single 'ERRATUM'.

It does seem right to say 'TERMINI'
Instead of 'TERMINUSES'
Though, not that they're reached by 'OMNIBI'
But, rather, several 'OMNIBUSES'.

One animal's a 'HIPPOPOTAMUS',
Two are 'HIPPOPOTAMI',
'HIPPOPOTAMUSES' makes a fuss,
Amongst grammarianii.

Some folk never mention a 'MEDIUM'.
But, even singularly, they say 'MEDIA',
It's often said by some heid bum,
Who doesn't see or hear or redia!

The barman's reply, when I asked him for a 'MARTINUS',
'Sir, it's a "MARTINI" you want, – Ahem!'
'I beg your pardon, my man – but, just between us,
Had I wanted two, I should have asked for them.'

A SOPS FABLE

From a circus, wintering in the countryside,
A lady zebra, a nearby farm espied,
With a picnic sannie of apple and date,
She sallied forth, to investigate.

The first animal met was a grazing sheep,
'Tell me, how do you earn your keep?'
'A BAA't spring time, to keep MEH cool,
The farmer shears and sells MEHEH wool.'

The next encounter; with a sturdy horse,
The self-same question was asked, of course.
'I'm harnessed up and can't say NEIGH,
I pull great loads of corn and hay.'

She now spoke to a clucking hen,
'Tell me, what do you do then?'
'Each-CLUCKING-day, if I'm-CLUCKING-able,
I lay a-CLUCKING-egg for the-CLUCKING-farmer's table.'

Said a brown-eyed cow, with coat like silk,
'I'm UDDERLY MOO-ved, to providing milk.'
Loud stamping and snorting, from a pen,
Attracted the zebra's attention, then.

A black bull, built like a barn-door,
Was pawing the straw-strewn, earthen floor.
From his nostrils clouds of steam arose,
Water dripped from the brass ring through his nose.
'You don't lay eggs, you don't grow wool,
You don't give milk, no cart you pull.
What DO you do? I must know why.'
To which, the bull bellowed this reply;
(With a sound like a great deep-throated cough.)
'I'll show you. If you get those pyjamas off!'

19

'What will she drink, I wonder?'
Thus the novice suitor might ponder,
But, those in the know,
Fill her up with PERNOD,
For 'ABSINTHE MAKES THE TART GROW FONDER'.

* * *

'Now that we are on our way,
Cheapo Airlines apologise for the delay.
The pilot was unhappy with the starboard jet,
And high criteria must be met.'
'So you changed the engine,' a punter said.
'No way! We changed the pilot instead!'

* * *

'I see that you have a wooden peg,
How did you come by that loss?'
'A German shell took off my leg,
As the River Rhine we tried to cross.'
'In place of your hand, you have a hook,
Was that sacrificed in the Reich's defeat?'
'No, it's just that I forgot to look,
When crossing over a busy street.'
'You've also lost your good right eye,
Was that when this accident took place?'
'No, that was a seagull, flying high,
That managed to drop one on my face.'
(To explain he performed a little mime.)
'I'd just had my hook for a week, at the time.'

A NEAR MS, OR THE MCP STRIKES BACK.

Whilst men micht pass a lawfu' act
Tae stop discrimination,
And ensure a lass'll no get sacked,
For feminine flirtation.

Still, I wid think that we've been had,
For though all men are brothers,
The sisterhood are unco' glad
Tae be mair equal than the others.

The lassies, through men's richt guidwill,
A wheen new rights ha'e gained,
But, bein' wily wimmen, still,
Auld privileges they've retained.

For parity wi' men they strive,
Equality's their intention,
But HE mun toil till SIXTY-FIVE,
Whilst, SHE at SIXTY, gets her pension.

Equal pay for equal work, they claim,
Because we too use our brains,
Then they're paid six months tae stay at hame,
Juist tae ha'e their weans.

If she'd a man but's noo alane,
She gets the widow's pension,
But if HE is left tae rear the wean,
He doesn't get a mention.

Though we can no' an advert cite,
For cellarMEN or barMEN,
Aye contrar' they maintain the right,
A woman must play CARMEN.

If she should steal frae C&A,
She's like tae get aff free,
Or fined a pound, wi' time tae pay,
It's blamed on PMT.

Another law that they escape,
('cos they ha'e chromosome X)
A woman can't be charged wi' rape,
So they don't want for sex.

Tae fair disguise her spinsterhood,
As MIZ she wid be kent,
But, when we see her wi' her brood,
Jalouse her nichts MIZspent.

So's no way possible tae be thought,
As objects o' a sexual kind,
(They're feart that ever they were caught,
Causin' corruption in men's mind.)

Their womanly charms they try tae hide,
And cover up their natural shapes,
Wi' gansies that are unco' wide,
An' frocks that hing like windae drapes.

O! The Guid Lord, made frae Adam's rib,
A blithe and bonny lass,
Why then, should freens o' wimmens lib
A' try tae look like a hoarse's ass?

* * *

SMALL ADS

Wooden hallstand, with mirror and pegs,
For sale by a lady with finely carved legs,
LOST – A three-legged dog, whose coat is yuckie,
He's got one eye and answers to LUCKY.

The ADS, FOR SALE, are getting seedier.
A book entitled *HOW to HUG*,
(That's volume four of the Encyclopaedia)
And, 'Two single beds – and a worn rug.'

* * *

'TREE FELLERS WANTED.' The forestry notice said.
As seen by two friends, Sean and Pat.
''Tis a pity Moichael stayed in bed,
Or us t'ree fellers could have apploied for dat.'

* * *

'You're married to one of identical twins,
How'd you tell them apart? They both look divine.'
'I can't tell the difference, for my sins,
But then, that's THEIR problem – not mine.'

* * *

'Dearest Mum,' wrote her sailor son,
'I'm forbidden to say where I've been,
But two weeks ago I had some fun,
I slept with a Geisha – know what I mean?
Last week we went – where you must not know,
But I shot a polar bear, in the snow.
I still can't divulge my present location,
But the nurses treat me with kind, loving care,
The doc says, if I'm ever in the same situation,
I should shoot the Geisha and sleep with the bear.'

* * *

The handsome doctor was very circumspect,
When taking girls' temperatures or tapping their knees,
But, just to allow for his own effect,
He always knocked off three degrees.

* * *

Two girls, in a rainstorm on Skye,
Made efforts to keep themselves dry.
'Is there a big mackintosh there,
To cover two lassies, fair?'
'No I'm a wee Campbell, but willing to try!'

* * *

Oedipus has taken the Freudian rap,
For bridging the generation gap.
He was no worse than many another,
Like a dutiful son, he loved his mother.

NATURAL DISASTERS

Jock, Pat and Taffy, somewhere abroad,
Were all facing death, by the firing squad.
Jock was the first to be placed at the wall,
But, at the last moment, gave out a loud call,
The word that he shouted was 'AVALANCHE!'
The soldiers fled, without a backward glance.

Taffy's tactics were just the same,
And as the troopers took their aim,
At the top of his voice, he called out 'FLOOD!'
The squad ran off, having shed no blood.
Thus, having learned from the Scotsman's jape,
Taffy, too, made good his escape.

Pat, impressed by the other two,
Now knew just what he had to do,
Disdaining a blindfold and a cigarette,
Stood, calmly, as the squad got set.
Just as they raised their rifles, higher,
With a smile on his lips, he shouted 'FIRE!'

* * *

A priest and a rabbi met on a train,
And Rev. looked at Rab. with a hint of disdain.
'As a Jew, to you, pork meat is denied?'
'It's against my religion.' the rabbi replied.
Said the priest, adopting a superior position,
'That seems like a rather bizarre superstition.'
'As a priest,' said the Jew, "You're forbidden to wed.'
'It's against my religion.' the priest smugly said.
On his head the Rabbi heaped fiery coals,
'It sure as hell beats bacon rolls.'

* * *

On the child psychologist's door was framed,
A notice for everyone to see,
In big, bold letters it proclaimed,
'GONE TO DIN-DIN, BACK AT FWEE.'

* * *

In fourteen-hundred and ninety-two,
Columbus sailed the ocean blue.
If, America, he hadn't found,
There'd be lots more Indians still around.

Said the nursery teacher, ever so sweet.
'You've got your shoes upon the wrong feet.'
Replied the tottering little tot,
'But these are the only feet I've got.'

CHAIN OF COMMAND or THE BUCK STOPS HERE

The intercom announced, with a voice like doom,
'Mr Smith will you please report to my room'.
The Managing Director crossed the floor,
And entered in at the Chairman's door.
A few minutes later, another call,
'We both wish to see you, Mr McFall.'
The accountant, looking rather blue,
Went to join the other two.
Again the instrument came to life,
In tones, which cut like a Stanley knife,
'Mr Watson, will you please come in!'
The Office Manager, managed a sickly grin.
The next to be summarily summoned,
The Senior Clerk, a Mr Drummond,
'We wish to see you, if you please!'
He approached the door, with trembling knees.
Then, came the call that he had feared,
The Office Boy, the sanctum, neared,
On entering, blushing, face aglow,
Was faced with the rest, in menacing row.
'Now, out with it boy – I want the truth,
Have you made love to my secretary, Ruth?'
Nervous before that corporate stare,
'N-N-No Sir, No – I wouldn't dare.'
'I believe you,' said the boss, 'as a matter of fact,
So YOU go and tell her that she's sacked.'

McGONAGALL ON THE NEW FORTH BRIDGE

Near Edinburgh is a brilliant view,
The Forth Road Bridge is spanking new,
Made of concrete and strong steel wires,
It is everything the heart desires.
It makes the drivers for to smile and laugh
Because it cuts the time in half,
You can leave Auld Reekie at half past three,
And be in Dundee in time for tea.
It is built so strong, it should not fall down,
But, if it did, the drivers would surely drown.
If, over the side, the car should crash,
It would hit the water with a mighty splash,
Of his bits and pieces, it could be said, in troth,
That he did multiply as he went Forth.

* * *

SAD, COUNTRY AND WESTERN FOLK SONG

Why do I cry, long into the night?
Why do I sigh, with all of my might?
Losing you, was the worst thing that's happened to me,
I'm footsore and weary as all here can see.
I search down the trails where we used to go,
I call out your name, as I search high and low,
You must know how much I miss you, of course,
Naught surpasses the love of a man for his horse.

As the nurse took the bedpan away from his bed,
The ailing town councillor, grinned, and he said,
'Though I've been on the council since before I married,
It's the first time I've ever had a motion carried.'

* * *

The PE teacher won renown,
Whilst getting boys to 'Jump up and down'.
Answering the demand for increased efficiency,
Considered it an ample sufficiency,
Giving his orders clear and well,
He just said, 'Jump up,' – they came down themsel'.

* * *

Catching grammarian hubby and housemaid in bed,
'John, I'm surprised,' his startled wife said.
Gently he, his wife, admonished.
'No Dear. *I* am surprised – *you* are astonished.'

* * *

The Chairman had a Girl Friday,
She assured his appointments would jell,
If his wife was away at her mother's,
He had her at weekends as well.

* * *

SCORED AT HOME

'I'd to go shopping with the wife, last Saturday,
That's why I missed Celtic's cup-tie away.'
Said his pal, 'I had that problem, too,
But, I found the answer, here's what you do:
If, on Saturday, she mentions shops,
Don't crudely smack her round the chops,
Just hustle her up the stairs, instead,
Throw her, face down, on the marital bed,
Let her know, to shopping, you're no' inclined,
Wi' a couple o' skelps on her bare behind.
That's the stuff to give the troops,
See you next week, to cheer on the "HOOPS".'

But, he was posted missing, again,
And had, his absence, to explain.
'I did exactly what you said,
Took her upstairs and on to the bed.
On my face I tried to keep a frown,
As her skirt went up and her pants came down,
I raised my hand, as you said I ought,
Over her pink -- and --- dimpled ---- bot—
Ach! well! there's not much more to say,
We were only playing Airdrie anyway.'

* * *

Could be trouble in Turkey any day,
If the Kurds don't get their whey.

A STITCH IN TIME . . .

If his sex life, still, is great,
Though his family numbers eight,
Into a private nursing home, he
Must go to have a vasectoemee.
This cut-price op was such a snip,
He can now afford to let things rip,
Continue sowing his oats, wild,
They spoiled the rod to spare the child.

* * *

SCANDALNAVIA

Finland's fussy,
Denmark's loose,
Sweden's sleazy,
But Norway SPRUCE.

OAK FIR YEW

They wail in Wales,
It's a Celtic sign,
The Irish keen,
But all Scots PINE.

THE FILO-FAX FANATIC

An organised young man, Filo-fax in hand,
Was stopped by a stranger, who adopted a stand.
'Before me is this Bob Burns I see?'
Without consulting his book, Bob said, 'That's me.'
'Did you go on holiday last year, in July?'
He looked up VACATIONS – 'That I won't deny.'
'Was it for two weeks – beginning the second?'
Consulting CALENDAR – 'Yes, that WAS when,' he reckoned.
'Did you fly, CALEDONIAN – Flight twenty-nine?'
From CONVEYANCE he confirmed, 'You're bang on the line.'
'Did you travel to Spain, to the Costa del Sol?'
Looking at LOCATIONS – 'You're right on the ball.'
'Did you have Room Fifteen, at the HOTEL del MAR?'
Reading RESIDENCES he replied – 'You are dead right, so far.'
'Did you meet a young lady whose first name was Bess?'
He looked under NAMES and he simply said 'Yes.'
'Did you dine in an intimate bar in Marbella?'
Under MEALS he agreed – they had eaten Paella.
'Did you two, then go dancing in a smart cabaret?'
ENTERTAINMENTS explained that he couldn't say 'Nay.'
'And back to the hotel to make love in your bed?'
SOCIAL CONTACTS concurred, 'It is quite true,' he said.
'You cad! You've the effrontery to agree!
She, Sir, is my wife. I don't like it, you see!'
He looked under COMMENTS and made this reply;
'I see that it says here, that neither did I.'

WHAT'S AFOOT ZEN?

Meditate upon legs,
'Til your mind goes "POP" '
You get to the bottom,
By going to the top.

SLIPPED FLOPPY DISC

Competition for computers,
Is a thought that galls,
Bill Gates thinks an abacus,
Is a load of old balls.

PRO BONO

To define lady lawyers,
For foreign visitors:
'Those with briefs, are barristers,
Those without, are solicitors.'

CARMA

Ruby, in her new 'ELAN',
Hailed a passing Buddhist chum,
He, an ardent Mantra fan,
Said, 'OM MANE PADME HUM.' *
* Translation:'Hail to the jewel in the Lotus.'

BAR L

'Dear Boys,' wrote Mum,
'For your new ranch,
I've got a name that's neat,
I think we'll call it "FOCUS",
For that's where THE SONS RAISE MEAT.'

* * *

The teacher read the mother's absence note;
'He'd diarrhoea through a hole in his shoes,' she wrote.
On the back more writing was appended,
(Though, obviously, not for her intended)
She'd used the page twice, indicating thrift,
A message for husband, coming off a late shift,
'Dinner in oven, soup in cup,
If you want sex later – wake me up.'

* * *

Little Jenny learned the Green Cross Code.
'Always look both ways before crossing the road.'
She did as bid, when in the town,
And, dutifully, looked up and down.

* * *

Greater love for music no man hath,
Than when a young lady, in her bath,
Starts to sing, and should he hear,
To the keyhole, applies his EAR.

Cleopatra clutched her breast,
As the snake, around her, curled,
They sang, as she was laid to rest,
'The biggest ASP-disaster in the world.'

* * *

The tenor thought he had made the right choice.
Marrying a hag, with a heavenly voice,
As she lifted her veil, having put on the ring,
One look and he snarled, 'Oh! for God's sake – SING!'

* * *

'Signor Bertolucci – Maestro Grand'
Announced the liveried flunkey.
'The greatest organist in the land.'
('til someone stole his monkey.)

* * *

TWO BEAUX TO HER STRING

He said, 'I won't play second fiddle,
That, you must understand.'
Said she, 'Considering your instrument,
You're lucky to be in the band.'

THE SCOT ABROAD

Roamin' in the gloamin'
On the Isle of Tenerife,
Where a' the brown young lassies,
Wear bikinis, mighty brief.
If you should chance tae see them,
When they're utterly undressed,
Just like roasted chicken,
A' the white bits are the best.

* * *

By yon bonnie banks and by yon bonnie braes,
Where the sun shines bright on Mallorca,
On the Algarve and Corfu and Benidorm too,
And on a' the wee hard men in Menorca.

* * *

'Speed bonnie plane, like a bird on the wing.
Duty-free hauf pints and nips.'
Merrily, hear the Scots punters sing,
'Here's tae paella an' chips.'

* * *

I love Alassio,
A town that's quite first classio,
I love Naples, Rome and Venice just as well,
It's the sweetness o' the weather,
The bonnie sunny weather,
And Glasgow – can go tae Hell!

* * *

'We're a' gaun tae Palma; That's oan Majorkee.
An' whit will we dae tae Palma?- Jist you wait an' see.
We're only a bunch o' young lager louts,
As anyone here can tell,
But, when we get a couple o' pints o' cerveza,
We make every yin else's life hell.'

* * *

'I've just arrived on the Isles of Greece,
Wi' a bag o' chips an' a jeely piece,
And I enquire of the local police,
Tonald – Where's the boozers?'

* * *

Keep right on to the Island of Rhodes,
Keep right on down to Crete,
Though the food is cool, the Taverna full,
Say 'Yasso' to all those you meet.
Though your eyes are bleary, keep drinking on,
Though your money may not last the week,
And all the friends you've been boozing with,
Will all find themselves up the Greek Creek.

* * *

The sight of a sanguine, setting sun,
Announces another day's route has run,
No bouquet there be, that bids so fair,
As night-scented stock, on the still twilit air.
Sweet the whirr of swallow wings, questing their nest,
To whit to woo of the owl, new-waked from his rest,
But – that evening sound, which all these doth surpass,
Is the tinkle of ice in a clear crystal glass.

* * *

BISHOP TAKES PORN – MATE

'Fifteen kids! – what a nice Catholic family,
More of that's what this diocese lacks.'
'They're not Catholics, My Lord,' said the curate.
'Then they're Protestant sex maniacs.'

* * *

'Your sixth set of twins, Mrs Murphy,
That must give you great pride to recall.
D'you get twins every time?' asked His Lordship.
'No – sometimes we get nothing at all.'

* * *

In the monastery, as in society,
The Rat Race does exist.
Instead of counting money,
They tot up beggars, kissed.

* * *

As the ingenuous young air-hostess says,
After working for just a few days,
In reply to the query,
'Are you in the MILE-HIGH CLUB, dearie?'
'I don't know – How high ARE Cathkin Braes?'

* * *

Folk have their own metabolic rate,
With sad results, I fear,
Wife dieting down to dress size eight,
Causes hubby to completely disappear.

* * *

'My complaint,' said the barmaid, in distress.
'Men come from that toilet, still adjusting their dress.'
'I can see nothing from the bar,' the landlord replied.
'But, if you stand on this crate and lean over to the side—'

* * *

Pouring her a liqueur, in his bachelor den,
(I might make this one, I think,)
'It's Cointreau, my dear, so just say "When".'
'Sure – right away after this drink.'

* * *

In a car crash, an Indian Fakir,
Said, 'Karma has brought this about.'
The other driver, it seems, was a Quaker.
'Screw thee friend!' he was heard to shout.

* * *

In the Outer Hebrides, the three islands of North Uist, Benbecula and South Uist are linked by causeways. N.Uist is predominantly Protestant, S.Uist is completely Catholic and Benbecula is nearly neutral.

A MISTY ISLES MORALITY TALE

In strict North Uist Donald dwelt,
A red-haired, raw-boned, Protestant Scot,
In softer South Uist, the home of the Celt,
Lived dark-eyed Morag, a Catholic, by lot.

Like Capulet and Montague,
Though religion kept them apart,
Blind Pantheist, Cupid, his love-bow drew,
And his arrows, ecumenic, pierced them to the heart.

More mundanely at a Saturday ceilidh,
Held on Benbecula's neutral strand,
They birled and hooched at the Gordons Gayly,
To Jimmy Shand's button-accordion band.

In a corner, sat the minister of the Wee Free Kirk,
The Reverend Hamish McKnight B.D. M.A.,
His attendance, a chore he did not shirk,
To ensure it ended ere the Sabbath Day.

Father O'Flaherty footed it featly,
A man of quite imposing girth,
Performing the intricate steps, quite neatly,
Rejoicing in the general mirth.

Sweating, as the weather was rather sultry,
'A wee whisky, Minister?' asked his soft Irish voice.
'Indeed not – I'd rather commit adultery.'
'Damn – I didn't know there was a choice!'

In spite of Hatfields and McCoys,
Don and Morag met in their secret place,
Girls being girls and boys being boys,
Their clandestine courtship grew apace.

At times, they almost gave up hope,
Due to incessant altercation,
John Knox pitted against the Pope,
Free Will versus Predestination.

Fortunes of football fixtures noted,
Counting the Cups and League Flags won,
Quarrels, quantitatively quoted,
Celtic Bhoys against Rangers Hun.

With extra spice, because it was banned,
And aware their parents it would vex,
Their 'MIXED MARRIAGE' was, in private, planned,
(To them, it meant persons of opposite sex.)

They tried to win their parents round,
From the pious platitudes their pastors preached,
Neither, gracefully, would give ground,
And so, a compromise was reached.

Depending on which foot they'd use to pass
In Church, the families sat left and right,
Father O'Flaherty said Nuptial Mass,
The sermon, lengthily, given by Mr.McKnight.

From the Vatican came a Blessing of note,
(Her uncle was on The Holy Rota.)
His brother lent his idle fishing boat.
He'd already filled his White Fish Quota.

United thus, female and male,
To each other they swore to be loyal,

Across the Minch, the two set sail,
For Mallaig and the Hotel Royal.

Later, alone in the Bridal Suite,
All problems appeared in the past,
Cosy, before a fire of peat,
Free to be themselves, at last.

Donald relished his wedding night,
As, modestly, Morag to the bathroom retired,
Reappearing, she set his eyes alight,
In the briefest of silken nighties attired.

'Be gentle with me, as you wreak your will.'
(Donald's face became a deeper red.)
'Because – I am a virgin, still.'
And spread herself on the nuptial bed.

Donald reacted to this news,
To him, it sounded the knell of doom,
In no time, he'd pulled on his trews,
And slammed the door, as he left the room.

Quickly to the quay and the fishing smack,
Smartly the stay-sail set aloft,
And, speedily, he made passage back,
To North Uist and his mother's croft.

Donald's demeanour was one of contrition.
'I've left her,' said he, and he hung his head.
'She's still a virgin, by her own admission.'
'You did right, my boy,' his mother said.

Hard lines set round her granite mouth,
And her chosen words were few,
'If she wasn't good enough for the Catholic boys of the South,
She's certainly not good enough for you.'

This married acrobatic team,
Stay together, as a matter of fact,
Although, twice nightly, it would seem,
He caught his wife in the act.

* * *

The actress had two red marks on her scapula.
She had a BIT part, in the film *DRACULA*.

* * *

ACCOUNTING FOR WOMEN was the new business course.
Expecting the class to be brimmin',
But it failed through lack of financial resource,
Men all know there's no accounting for women!

* * *

In his uniform, as Admiral of the Fleet,
Phillip and the Queen went to Portsmouth town.
The Mayor was there, his guests to greet,
And the Town Clerk's job was to show them aroun'.
Going to see a new-built council flat,
'We'll visit Number Two,' The Town Clerk said.
(They'd been warned to provide a welcome mat.)
But, missing Two A, went to Two B instead.
The door was opened by a little waif,
Her dirty face held a welcome grin,
'Mammy said it would be quite safe,
Even though she isn't in.
Mam said' – Meanwhile the Town Clerk glares –
"If a woman comes here with a sailor, Mabel,
Tell her to use the room upstairs,
And leave five pounds on the bedside table".'

* * *

The feisty young blonde in the jazz bar,
Had a theory she put to the test,
She'd eat only a third of a Mars Bar,
'Who the hell wants to work and to rest?'

* * *

A survey by sociologists done,
Its conclusions were rather desultory,
In discovering which ones had more fun,
Infants in infancy, or adults in adultery.

* * *

Before the days of HARD HATS being generally worn shipyard foremen always wore bowler hats. This served two purposes: it was the badge of their authority and it afforded protection from a red-hot rivet, inadvertently dropped from high up on the ship's side just as he was passing underneath.

TRADITION DIES HARD

Young Senga was a modern Miss,
And only did what she wanted to,
She'd only kiss those whom she wished to kiss;
If you didn't like it – 'TOUGH! – STUFF YOU!'

She was prepared to work quite hard,
A career, she valued above all other,
She wanted a job in the local yard,
To be a shipwright, like her brother.

And, thus it was, with this in view,
She presented herself to the shipyard doorman,
To say she had an interview,
With Mr.McSkimmin, the senior foreman.

His bothy was by the fitting-out quay.
To her, he tipped his bowler hat.
'That's a sexist thing,' said she,
'We don't want any more of that.'

A note, on the board behind McSkimmin,
Said 'Irrespective of the effects,
All jobs should be open to women,
Absolutely regardless of sex.'

'So you want to learn a trade,' said he,
'There'll be no time for high-heels or frocks,

Or any other such fripperee,
When climbing the side of a ship on the stocks.

'Standard Grade Geography, Latin and French,
Home Economics and English are past,
They should be useful, when wielding a wrench,
A comfort when sixty feet up on a mast.'

'I know, at times, things will be bad,
But I'm here to see it through.
I can compete with any lad,
And I'll do anything they can do.

'I'll learn to drink tea from a can,
Play football at the mid-day break,
Succeed to swear, like any man,
And write a bookie's line, to stake.

'I'll fight o'er favourite football teams,
And boast the conquests I have made.
(I know that most are in their dreams,)
Take umbrage at each thing that's said.

'With dirty nails and smelly feet,
As each, adolescent, spot deploys,
With all of this I will compete,
I'll be the Boiliest of the boys.'

'I'm sure, the techniques, you can handle,
Learn of pulley, block and cleat,
The job will not be worth the candle,
There's one thing which might you defeat.

'With men it has always been a condition,
(And no intent of sexual *har*assment.)
To undergo a passing-out tradition,
Which might cause you acute embarrassment.

'This may come as quite a shock,
But their bums are belted by a tarry rope,
They then swim, naked, across Govan Dock.'
'No probs,' said she, 'With that I'll cope.'

'Ere you're awarded the tools of your trade,
Comes the test of the SHIPWRIGHT ALE,
With all the apprentices on parade,
And this is where I fear you'll fail.

'Before you get your set-square and bevel,
You have to drink three pints of beer,
Then standing up – and from ground level,
You have to pee over that wall, from here.'

* * *

At a bus-stop, just outside a house of ill-fame,
Jock, Pat and Abbie, were waiting until a bus came.
As they stood there, a minister, dressed all in black,
Came hurrying out, without looking back.
Patrick and Abraham turned upon Jock,
'That would sure scandalise his faithful flock.'
A few minutes later, with black hat and beard,
Through the same door, a rabbi appeared.
Said Pat, 'The congregation would be agog,
If they knew of this conduct at his synagogue.'
Some time after, five minutes, at least,
Out of the house came a small Catholic priest.
Cried Pat – 'ere the others could gloat their fill –,
'Sure wan o' them poor hooers must be ill.'

* * *

48

Abe Lincoln, addressing a jury in court,
Said, 'Things don't always seem as they ought.
You may have all the facts, without exclusion,
But still arrive at the wrong conclusion.'
This he emphasised in his peroration,
Using a rural scene, as an illustration:
A little girl called to her farmer dad,
'Pop! ah jest saw sumthin' awful bad,
It wur sister Suzy an' Hiram Brown,
Her skirts wuz up an' his pants wuz down.
They wur in the barn, acrost the way,
Ah 'spect they'se agoin' to pee on the hay.'

* * *

In the Garden of Eden, Eve stood by the gate,
Berating her Adam for coming home late.
He knew it was no use telling fibs,
For all she did was count his ribs.

* * *

A couple who'd both been married before,
Were blessed with children of their own,
Said Daddy to Mummy, 'Though you I adore,
Your kids and my kids won't leave our kids alone.'

* * *

Three applicants for work as a lighthouse keeper,
Were each asked how they'd pass their time,
In the long lonely nights, as winter got deeper,
And the warning buoy rang its monotonous chime.

The first was of a literary bent.
'I'd take crosswords and Scrabble and games of that sort,
To improve my vocabulary is my intent.'
The panel seemed pleased with this smart retort.

The next was not so mentally inclined,
He had lowered his pastime sights,
A dartboard and dominoes he had in mind,
To while away those endless nights.

Said the third 'I'll take TAMPAX to those barren rocks,
'And that would provide for my every whim,
"With TAMPAX" it says, right here on the box,
"You can dance or cycle, play tennis or swim.".'

* * *

Ellis Island, at the mouth of the Hudson, stands
Just a ferry ride from the Battery.
Here came foreigners seeking new lands,
IMMIGRATION'S THE SINCEREST FORM OF FLATTERY.

* * *

A woman to her consternation,
Found odd hairs growing on her doggy pet,
It was a Mexican Hairless, not an Alsatian,
So off to the chemist's shop she set.

'Can I have a strong hair remover,' she begs.
The chemist handed her a box,
'Rub this carefully on your legs,
But don't wear stockings, tights or socks.'

'It's not for my legs I want the stuff,
It's for my Chihuahua a cure I seek.'
'Right!' said the chemist, 'Fair enough,
But stay off your bike, at least for a week.'

* * *

'Have you anything to say? Before judgment is passed'
Asked the judge, of the man in the dock.
'Bugger all!' he rapped out fast,
But the deaf judge didn't hear him talk.

'What did he say?' he asked the Clerk of the Court.
'So, a sentence, I may approve.'
'He said "Bugger all",' was his retort.
'Strange – I was sure I saw his lips move.'

* * *

The unlucky jockey,
Broke his arm in two places,
At the Epsom Derby,
And the Cheltenham races.

POET'S PARADISE

What bliss it is,
Each and every time,
To find words
With reason, rhythm and rhyme!

* * *

It's known amongst the Inuit,
A fact they'll readily admit,
Even the best constructed igloos,
Don't have either small or big loos.
Eskimo folklore lets kids know,
'Never eat the yellow snow!'

'Tell me Donuil. Tell me true.
Tell me Donuil, Oh! Donuil Dhu,
Did ancient Scotsmen use a sea-loch,
Or did their wee broch have a pee-broch?'

* * *

To assess the approaching aircraft's condition,
Ground control said, 'Report your height and position.'
The pilot, who thought himself a clown,
Replied, 'Five foot nine and I'm sitting down.'

WISH I HAD A RIVER

I wish I had a river,
Just like the Rhine or Rhône,
I wish I had a river
To call my very own.
To have the Rhône, for me alone, would be a fine design,
But, better yet if Fate would let the River Rhine be mine.

I wish I had a Scottish river,
Just like the Tweed or Don,
Wish I had a Scottish river
And take the salmon ere they spawn.
In catching them, I would take care what clothing I should don,
I'd wear a Mac to cover up the Tweed suit I had on.

Wish I had an English river,
Like the Ribble or the Ouse,
Wish I had an English river
Whose water I could use.
To booze from the Ouse, I would strictly refuse,
No dribble from the Ribble, my tea will ever infuse.

Wish I had a French type river
Just like the Somme or Seine,
Wish I had a French type river
And the vineyards, which they drain.
Lack of sleep, the doctors say, can influence the brain,
So if you are in-Somme-niac you may end up in-Seine.

Wish I had a German river,
Like the Weser or the Ruhr,
Wish I had a German river
And was a wealthy German brewer.
I'd take the water from the stream and mash it with the grain,
And after drinking, it would go, back in the river once again.

Wish I had a neat Swiss river
Like the Danube or the Inn,
Wish I had a neat Swiss river
Clean as any brand-new pin.
The prissy Swiss go out each day and polish them with Min,
For even just a speck of dust, is thought a mortal sin.

Wish I had a Spanish river
Like the old Guadalquivir,
The trouble with Spanish rivers is,
They tend to disappear.
Looking at this river is embarrassing, I fear,
For owing to the climate, its bottom's bare all year.

Wish I had an Italian river
Like the Arno or the Po,
Wish I had an Italian river
Bathed in rosy Tuscan glow.
Florence sits on the Arno – art treasures all on show,
Who sits? What shows? On the other one, I do not wish to know.

Wish I had a Russian river
Like the Volga or the Yen,
Wish I had a Russian river
I'd eat caviar again.
The virgin sturgeon needs no urgin' to lay her eggs, but,
note then,
Blushes redly, when observed by all those very Volga boatmen.

Wish I had a Polish river
With a quite dyslexic name,
With C's and Z's and R's and K's
All sounding just the same.
An invitation to Gdansk, I'd eagerly acclaim,
Where ships and Solidarity did Liberty proclaim.

A BANK OF OARS

Sandra and her pals, all strapped for cash,
Decided to give street-walking a bash,
Mini-skirted and looking pretty,
They each chose different parts of the city.
At eleven, Sharon returned, unfrayed,
With the hundred and twenty pounds she'd made.
A tired Tracey came back at one,
Her earnings amounting to the ton.
They both hung on 'til ten to four,
When Sandra staggered through the door,
For a seat and a drink she really yearned,
Displayed the five pounds, ten pence she'd earned.
'That total doesn't make much sense,
Who, on earth, gave you that ten pence?'
Said Sandra, as, sleepily, her head nodded,
'As a matter of fact, I think they a' did.'

* * *

THE SOUND OF MUSIC

Wonderful singers, the Family von Trapp,
The reason, never revealed before,
They had to sing each day, as they had a crap.
(There was no lock on the lavvy door.)

Having clobbered the ned,
As only Cantona can,
It may truly be said,
That the merde hit the fan.

* * *

As is told in biblical lore,
Eve's botanical cover was brief,
I reckon all that Adam wore,
Was a hole in that fig leaf.

* * *

The boss's message was very clear,
'This firm's salesmen are all real do'ers,
The rest have upped their sales this year,
So, what I'm saying is, UP YOURS!'

* * *

Breaking wind, the teacher tried shifting the blame,
The loud report embarrassed her so.
'Stop that! – You— Whatever your name.'
'Certainly, Miss, which way did it go?'

* * *

THE IDEAL WIFE

This description is a rule of thumb,
She's blonde, pneumatic, deaf and dumb,
A nympho, who happens to own a pub,
Right at the gates of a posh golf club.

* * *

His Lordship, the Bishop, in vestments attired,
Pronounced the vicar and his housekeeper, fired,
He issued an 'Act of Ecclesiastic Sequestry,'
Finding his VEST in her PANTRY and her PANTS in his VESTRY

Over a vasectomy, there's no need to blubber,
With no lead in your pencil, you don't need a rubber.

* * *

A man entered a pub, and on the bar-top stuck,
A biscuit-tin, on which, stood a snow-white duck,
And, as the landlord looked askance,
Slowly, the duck began to dance.
At first, with neat and measured pace,
A waltz, performed with languid grace,
Then as if to say, 'Here's how I can go,'
Gave what passed for an Argentine Tango.
A polka, next, did the crowd amaze,
Recalling the Goose Step of previous days,
This was followed by a quickstep,
Necessitating a nifty trick step,
The footwork, elegant and classy,
With two reverse turns and a triple chassée.
The landlord saw the duck's potential,
His profits could be exponential,
This performance was sure to score,
The pub would be bulging at the door.
'Would you sell him to me for fifty quid?'
The man said he could and would and did.
As the duck continued with his mime,
He asked, 'How do I stop him at closing time?'
'Easy,' said the man, 'He's not hard to handle,
Just lift up the lid – and blow out the candle.'

* * *

For the altered Mass Card, I take the blame,
Using 'DOMESTOS' to erase the celebrant's name,
I think that this, at the very least,
Is a clear cut case of BLEACH OF THE PRIEST.

* * *

The nursery teacher addressed her little band,
'To go to the toilet, you must raise your hand.'
Said one little boy, with his hand at his crotch,
'No Miss, I don't need to, --- WATCH!'

* * *

'Thank you, God,' said the Swiss, 'for gifts like these,
Green pastures, cattle, rich milk and cheese.
God, try a glass of milk, it's straight from the cow.'
'Delicious,' said God.'What would you like now?'
Said the Swiss, who are noted for being thrifty,
'With VAT, that will be just one franc fifty.'

* * *

I like Swiss cheeses quite a lot,
They really are a model,
One characteristic they have got,
They do not HUM they YODEL.

* * *

59

Chicken Pilaff?
That sounds nice,
Must be Greek,
PART-HEN-ON rice.

* * *

The chemist went right over the top,
When told of the break-in at his shop,
Of all his stock, he was bereft,
Only packets of condoms and combs were left.
The police, who got there rather quick,
Are looking for a baldy Catholic.

* * *

You've never heard of these, I'll bet a fiver,
Whistler's FATHER, GRANDPA Moses and LORD Godiva.

* * *

East Enders, Corrie, Home and Away,
Neighbours and Emmerdale Farm,
On the soap packet, the warning should say,
'Watching these can do you severe mental harm!'

* * *

THE YUPPIE ANTHEM
A TRADE CYCLE GILTS GURU

Daisy, Daisy, make us our fortunes do!
Corporation balance-sheets, are meat and drink to you.
Voting shares and debentures,
Seem like romantic adventures,
And you'll look fair, upon the chair,
Of a company, entre nous.

Footsie, Footsie, please keep on climbing higher,
May ex-dividend equities all find a willing buyer.
The issue of fresh liquidity,
Means an end to fiscal rigidity,
One shouldn't knock a firm standing stock,
For it's that to which we all aspire.

Daisy, Daisy, how do your assets grow?
With BP and ESSO and pretty SHELL all in a row.
A bit of insider dealing,
As oil shares hit the ceiling,
And a tranche (That's a slice) at a give-away price,
Puts old port in your portfolio.

Daisy, Daisy, give us your answer, do!
Why is the floor of the Stock Exchange just like a lively zoo?
With STAGS and BULLS and BEARS,
Laying deposits down on shares,
I am quite sure, a deal in manure,
Is a knockout – a proper DUNG FU'.

* * *

A sleep so deep, produce it must,
A snore to shake the rafter,
Is this the famed sleep of the just?
Or the sleep of the just after.

* * *

With an appetite never quite satient,
Nurse Jones was a caution, it's said,
For she could make the patient,
Without disturbing the bed.

* * *

Birthdays and Christmas, supply the bread,
But Greetings Card makers shout, 'Hooray!'
For this provides the jam, to spread,
As punters plump for, 'Mother's Day.'

* * *

The Kennel Club gave the dog breeder fits,
Who crossed a Pit Bull and Labrador for a caper,
His aim, a dog that gave you the shits,
And then ran off with the toilet paper.

* * *

Laughter Lines

For the English ex-pats in Los Gigantes on Tenerife

L ots of post-yuppie things to see,
O ld Sloane Rangers in near nudity.
S uperannuated tax defectors,

G olden handshake,
I nsurance collectors,
G arden suburb,
A broad in the sun,
N obody's under seventy-one.
T hatcherites,
E nduring sun and sea,
S urrey, is where they'd rather be.

* * *

Crime is the worst of lower class diseases,
Defined as, anything the upper class displeases.

* * *

GENERATION GAP

PC Plod, near the end of his evening beat,
Looked forward to resting his weary feet,
His 'Eight to Twelve', was nearly done,
Time, though, to spoil someone's fun.
Down Lover's Lane, half-hid from view,
A four wheel love-nest, built for two,
There, in the midst of Love's Arena,
The Rep's Revenge – a Ford Cortina.
Condensation the car's interior hid,
Foiling a viable, voyeur's bid.
With a 'What's all this, then?' mighty roar,
Quickly threw open the nearside door,
No need for powers of deduction,
To see the scene set for seduction.
Handbrake to the floor, seats fully reclined,
Revealed what the occupants had in mind.
Gear lever, forward and pushed to the right,
(Avoids snagging a lowered trouser or tight,)
A 'packet of three' on the dashboard, handily,
Sinatra singing on the stereo, randily,
Babychams, for increased anticipation,
Or, for afters, in celebration.
And there, forecasting the final issue;
A box of absorbent, man-size tissue,
But – most surprising – when inspected,
Just space, where bodies were expected.
There, on the seats, with fun-fur covers,
A lack of lustful lungeing lovers,
But, see, in the back seat, quietly sitting,
He, with his book and she, with her knitting,
Instead of being *In Delicto, Flagrante*,
As perjink, as if having tea with their aunty.
Nonplussed and flustered, the PC demanded,
The question that his rule-book commanded.

(Pencil licked for the next blank page,)
Have you Insurance, Licence and what's your age?'
'Yes – to both and I'm twenty,' the boy replied.
'And how old's the young lady, by your side?'
'She's sixteen . . .' and looking at his watch, he reckons,
'In just seven minutes and fifteen seconds.'

Man progresses from INFANCY through ADOLESCENCE,
To ADULTERY and then to OBSOLESCENCE.
'Life begins at Forty,' is a dread shout,
For all will wear out, fall out or spread out.

* * *

From the bowlful, Dr. Paisley, picked up a dried petal,
'You've made a grave mistake I fear,
Take this away – and grasp the nettle.
We maintain, we'll have no 'POT POURRI' here.'

* * *

The praises of the, new-published, series, were sung,
Refresher courses on each CELTIC tongue,
BRUSH UP YOUR CORNISH, BRUSH UP YOUR BRETON,
These were books they were willing to bet on.
But with IRISH GAELIC – went into reverse.
Didn't fancy the title – *BRUSH UP YOUR ERSE*.

* * *

Said the sergeant, 'All soldiers will take their seats,
The officer's comin' to lecture on KEATS,
You'll all behave as if it's *been* fun,
Though you wouldn't know a KEAT – even if you seen one.'

DELICACY IS DERMATIC
OR
BEAUTY IS SKIN DEEP

On the train from Glasgow to Inverness,
I was faced with a vision of loveliness,
The perfect proportions of her face,
Bespoke a Botticelli Grace.
Her high cheekbones, enhanced by blusher,
Her lips like cherries, even lusher,
A flawless foundation her complexion,
Great violet eyes reveal my reflection.
Her wrists and arms, elegantly slim,
A cream silk blouse, filled to the brim,
Fine hands, long fingers, tipped with scarlet,
Her legs would shame a film starlet.
Her scent, a delicate hint of musk,
Her hair new-done by Rita Rusk,
Her svelte black suit, a Chanel rag,
Her Gucci shoes matched her Gucci bag.
As we sped through each Highland pass,
My thoughts sped to that lovely lass,
But, as we passed each awesome peak,
I was too much in awe to speak.
As we approached our destination,
To look her best for her assignation,
With consummate grace, she left her seat,
And, with steps, both lithe and neat,
Leaving me lovelorn by the view,
Moved magically towards the carriage loo.
With feet that barely touched the floor,
I followed to that toilet door,
Picturing a wishful situation,
'ENGAGED' had a different connotation.
In my mind's eye, I saw her stand,
Before the mirror, comb in hand,

Flick a stray hair into place,
Fuss with a frankly, faultless face.
Darken an eyelash, the better to flirt,
Straighten a seam, tug down a skirt.
Finally she came through that door,
Fairer, even than she'd been before,
She looks at me and my legs go weak,
And then my angel starts to speak.
'Before you go in, if I were you,
I think I'd wait a minute or two.'
Dabs a perfect nose with a lace-edged hanky,
'The guff in there is effin' manky.'

* * *

As the egotistical, Scots poet said,
'Burns and Scott and Macdiarmid are dead.
And speaking, personally, for myself,
I'm not feeling in the best of health.'

* * *

A Polish tourist had pains in his head,
So went to have his eyes tested.
'Please read the chart,' the optician said.
'Read it! – I *know* him!' he protested.

* * *

The born-again Christian, 'phoned the doc in distress,
'Did I leave my pants there, on resuming my dress?
As you know I'm a Seventh Day Adventist,
What shame, if I've left them at the dentist!'

* * *

Bungee jumping began with female doubt,
According to parachutists' lore,
Hesitating, when told she should bale out,
Caught her suspenders on the aircraft door.

* * *

A young Norse god, both lean and lithe,
Wooed a Snow-maiden, bonny and blithe,
As is told in folklore,
He said, 'I am Thor.'
'Tho am I,' said she, 'But it'th nithe.'

* * *

PRIORITY TREATMENT

A lady visitor from the Local Health Board,
Addressed the first man in a three bed ward,
'I'm here to see what I can do,
Tell me – what is troubling you?'
He gives a couple of embarrassed smiles,
'Well it's – er – you see – I suffer from piles.'
'What does the nurse do for that nasty complaint?'
'Twice daily, with iodine, my piles she'll paint.'
'I hope that brings you some relief.
I grant requests, as part of my brief.'
'I like doing crossword puzzles,' he said,
'A book of these would be welcome by my bed.'
'I'll arrange that,' said she, and spoke to the second.
'My complaint is exactly the same,' he reckoned.
The treatment he considered fine,
Having them painted, daily, with iodine.
His pleasure, he said, was Mills & Boon,
She promised to have some delivered quite soon.
The third man sounded a different note,
Huskily he said, he had a bad throat,
With his treatment, he made her acquainted,
Twice daily, with iodine, his tonsils were painted.
'I'm sure that treatment is of the best,
Now do you have a little request?'
Hoarsely, the words came out in a rush,
'Will you see that I get first shot of the brush?'

* * *

At the sea-front two pensioners sat on a seat,
Said Jim, 'I'll get something from the ice-cream van.'
'Alright,' said Jack, 'Now you're on your feet,
Try to remember this, if you can.
I'll have a vanilla ice-cream pokey hat,
With hundreds and thousands on the top,
And raspberry sauce poured over that,
A chocolate flake and a bottle of pop.
Are you sure you'll get the message right?
I don't want to be unkind,
At your age you're not quite so bright.'
'No bother, I'll keep it all in mind.'

He returned with two full bags of chips.
'I said your memory was fickle,'
Said his friend, as he put one to his lips,
'You've just forgotten the Branston pickle.'

* * *

Said Daniel to Abraham, 'Sad to tell,
One of my brothers is far from well.'
'Oh! Is 'e ?'
'No – Ikey.'

* * *

Fear in a parachute jump I found,
Something I wouldn't do again,
I was not just relieved as I reached the ground,
I'd relieved myself as I left the 'plane.

MUSLIN' IN

Bill, a pillar of his community,
Turned up on Monday with a ripe black eye,
Denied a hint of office immunity,
He had to give the reason why.

'Yesterday in church, I sat behind
A lovely lass with a muslin dress,
A delicate fabric – quite unlined,
The heat, soon started to oppress.

At the end of the service, as we all arose,
I couldn't resist a couple of peeks,
To see the skirt of her sweat wet clothes,
Lodged between her bottom's cheeks.

'Being the gentleman that I am,
I leaned over to find what the answer might be,
And, meaning not a bit of harm,
Tweaked the garment, to set it free.

'My action wasn't taken kindly,
She turned and fixed me with a glare,
Then with her fist, she lashed out blindly,
And,' pointing to his eye, 'Hit me, right there.'

The next Monday, to everyone's surprise,
And causing considerable consternation,
Bill turned up with TWO black eyes,
All were agog for his explanation.

'Although of women I've known a few,
I can't understand them, I must confess,
Yesterday, in the very same pew,
Was the same lovely lass in the same muslin dress.

'If anything, the weather was even warmer,
And, naturally, she'd started to perspire,
So the same thing happened to this charmer,
Her dress gripped in – but even higher.

'Memory told me not to act,
But my sister, who beside me stood,
MY experience sadly lacked,
And thought the situation rude.

'She'd experienced the same upon her bike.
She pulled it out, thinking praise to win,
But this, I knew she did not like,
So – extending a finger – I poked it back in.'

That age-old question over which men natter,
Is it true what they say that size doesn't matter?
Leon Goosen's bassoon is bigger than a flute,
But James Galway doesn't give a toot!

* * *

We must believe in Free Will,
We've no choice – for what's the odds,
That the Doctrine of Monotheism,
Is surely a gift from the gods.

* * *

Two caterpillars, munching leaves on a twig,
Of dew-drops taking the occasional swig,
High above, in the clear blue sky,
A bright coloured butterfly fluttered by,
One caterpillar raised his hairy head,
'You wouldn't get me up in one of those things,' he said.

* * *

FILLOSOPHY

Wearing trousers, you might be taken to task,
As a lady of rather ample means.
The Jesuitic viewer, might well ask,
'Does your END quite justify your JEANS?'

'Technical training' has replaced 'Education'

'Tech training is the greatest thing, bar none,
Let me tell you what I've so far done:
About this time last year,
I couldn't SPELL "Engineer",
Now, would you believe it, I ARE one.'

* * *

A gynaecologist, whose methods were heterodox,
Would shun those 'We'll soon make you better' talks.
Showing off, for a caper,
He'd scrape, paint and paper,
The walls of his hall, through the letter-box.

* * *

It's fu' grand shairly,
Tae retire airly,
An' face life wi' a grin.
A year o' days, tae sleep an' laze,
And aye the pension comin' in.

* * *

The girl cheated in 'Human Biology' tests,
As she was seen to count her breasts.

* * *

THE COARSE NUN'S CHORUS

Novice nun Angela's background was poor,
Deserted Mum – and her Dad? – she wasn't quite sure.
With six other kids in a room and kitchen,
Damp walls and bed-bugs that started you itchin',
Her environment, dominated by noise,
With four younger sisters and two rowdy boys.

One day a visiting nun at school,
Told of her Order's monastic rule,
Silence, maintained in every way,
Save for one half hour a day.
The space and quiet of a convent cloister,
Appeared to her like the pearl in an oyster.

So, having donned her habit and wimple,
Life for her became tranquil and simple.
Sadly, one trait she did not leave behind,
On rare occasions she'd still eff and blind,
In moments of stress, though these were few,
She'd still come out with a swear word or two.

Said the Mistress of Novices, 'You MUST understand,
Here, the very *mildest* expletive is banned.
I know, at times we can all be crabbit,
But you must stop this – or get out of the habit.'
This was a conventional convent joke,
Which mild smiles would evoke.

She tried, very hard, to think of her Saviour,
And was a model of perfect behaviour,
Unfortunately, one day, in the refectory,
With Reverend Mother reading at the lectuary,
Sister Angela, bringing soup to the table,
Tripped over a loose electric cable.

The soup splattered over the seated sisters,
(The subsequent source of sinister blisters)
And Sister Angela, as she fell,
In sheer frustration, yelled out 'HELL!
OH! SHIT! – I said HELL! – OH! HELL! – I said SHIT!
OH! BUGGER! I'm better, EFFIN' WELL, out of it.'

* * *

The dyslexic, Devil worshipper,
Was open to banta'
He made a pact,
And sold his soul to SANTA.

* * *

Most grafitti are anti-Catholic in scope.
The reason – though others are NOT banned,
It IS much easier to write 'F— THE POPE,'
Than 'F— THE MODERATOR OF THE GENERAL ASSEMBLY
OF THE FREE CHURCH OF SCOTLAND.'

* * *

Before I departed to the Crusade,
For my wife a chastity belt was made.
The key joined the others on the chain,
Of my aged butler who had to remain.
I'd just gone, when he hobbled after me,
'Sire! Sire! You've left the wrong key.'

A young girl who read 'bodice-rippers,'
Had boy-friends, all 'Stiff upper-lippers.'
Down Love's Lane, in the dark,
Said, 'To the crickets, pray hark.'
'Not crickets,' said he, 'those are zippers.'

* * *

Angler Noah had to come to terms,
After catching two fish, he had run out of worms.

* * *

Said the Duke to a friend, about the grub,
At the Annual Dinner of his Polo Club,
'As for the melon, I have to say,
Had it been as cold as the consommé,
If that soup, on which we were to dine,
Had been as warm as the white table wine,
If the wine had been as old as the chicken,
And the chicken as young and finger-lickin'
As the pretty waitress, wearing MUCH less,
And had she been as willing as the Duchess,
Then the grace, "So may the Lord be thankit",
Might well have applied to this bum banquet.'

* * *

SECURITY LEAK

Spies X and Y at the MI5 ball,
Y took X's arm, as they entered the hall.
(It seemed a secret signal was given,
As M nodded curtly, to Double Oh Seven.)
'May I have this dance X?' Y asked, politely,
And, taking the floor, waltzed deftly and lightly.
'Shall we sit this one out X?' he said, holding her hand.
'A spot, undercover, where we still hear the band.'
'May I get you a drink X?' was his next request.
'Martini, shaken, not stirred, with a lemon for zest.'
But, as they were leaving, gave the game away,
'May I help you on with your coat – eh – Miss Grey?'

* * *

To the taxidermist went a real old dearie,
With her dead, pet chimps – from foreign lands.
'Would you like them mounted?' was his query,
'No, I think I'd prefer them just holding hands.'

* * *

Stranded on an iceberg, they waved and waved,
The two explorers were starting to panic.
Then, one called out, 'We're saved! We're saved!
Look! Here comes the *Titanic!*'

* * *

At a wartime anti-aircraft site,
Lady guests were welcomed on Friday night.
Entertaining a visitor from the ATS
In the Nissen hut used as the officers mess,
A rubber of bridge was then proposed,
And round the table, a four composed.
As Senior Officer, at his own behest,
The Colonel, with the lady, would play East and West.
In responding to his partner's call,
His bidding wasn't good, at all,
Although he'd read up on his Hoyle,
His partner's contracts he would spoil.
In working out Hand Valuation,
He'd give out faulty information,
And, leave them both in serious trouble,
By bidding into a Penalty Double,
In every hand they had to play,
His Point Count would lead her astray.
He'd murmur, 'Very sorry, Ma'am,'
When failing badly in a slam.
The North-South pair were doing fine,
With points above and below the line.
Having left his partner in a fog,
'Must go,' said the Colonel, 'See man about dog.'
But, instead of making his way to the loo,
Thought the outside wall of the hut would do.
The stream, against iron corrugation,
Set up a strong reverberation,
Inside the noise was amplified,
Apologies the younger officers tried.
The lady, however, was quite unfazed,
And left the others real amazed,
To hear her say, in sheer delight,
'This is the turning point of the night,
It's the very first time, you understand,
That I know, for sure, what he has in his hand.'

* * *

TRUNK CALL

An elephant who'd wandered off from a zoo,
In a village created quite a to-do,
He paused to feed himself on greens,
In the garden of a lady, with some "frien's."
Having never seen one of these before,
She commented on it, from her back door.
'Oot here's this muckle, great grey beast,
He must be a dozen feet, at least.
He's goat nae heid, but a huge long tail,
Wi' it he's pullin' oot cabbages an' kail,
The sicht ye could'nae well conceive,
Whit he's daein' wi' them, ye wid'nae believe.'

* * *

Asked the bride and groom, as to church they were heading,
'Does he believe in sex before the wedding?'
The vicar's answer to them was relayed,
'Not if the ceremony is delayed.'

* * *

The vicar's wife, in sex, sought a bit of variety.
'But I only know one position, Mary,
As an active member of the "Bible Society",
I am, after all, a missionary.'

* * *

The blushing bride looked very pretty,
As she took her wedding vow,
A notice outside said 'Don't throw confetti –
And, BRETHREN, this means THOU!'

* * *

We'll publish, regardless of cost, then,
In a textured morocco binding,
Your novel, *Persuasion*, Miss Austen,
If you'll cut out the effing and blinding.

* * *

The Grand Duke von Hapsburg won undying fame,
When asked to a recent Austria – Hungary game.
He made football history by simply saying,
'Of course I'll come, but who are we playing?'

IN CONVENIENCE

Said the lavatory attendant, 'This job has changed,
It's not what it used to be.
The folk who come in are all deranged,
They're not in here to pee.
Thieves come in to Divvy-up,
Drunks are here to be sick,
Winos will come, their booze to sup,
Junkies themselves with needles stick.
If, just for a crap, someone came down that stair,
To me, it would seem like a breath of fresh air.'

* * *

The eminent surgeon worked without pause,
(His students relished the gore)
As his Heart/Lung transplant gained applause,
Took out the appendix – as an encore.

* * *

Doctor O'Leary made his name,
And won a first-class reputation,
His work earned him undying fame,
He specialised in appendix transplantation.

* * *

A lady at the psychiatrist's door,
Met a friend who'd been there before,
'Tell me, are you coming or going, my dear?'
'If I knew that, I wouldn't be here.'

* * *

'To cheer myself up, I get a new hat,
Whenever I'm down in the dumps,' said she.
Says hubby, 'I'm glad to find out that,
Where you got them from always puzzled me.'

* * *

Said the man from the Pru, 'We won't give you cash,
We'll replace the missing item, for life.'
This news, the husband, did rather abash,
'Will you cancel the policy on the wife?'

* * *

His arithmetic wasn't good enough,
Even to play pontoon for fun.
He had to strip down to the buff,
If he wanted to count to twenty-one.